Also by Selwyn Hughes
in this series
The Divine Eagle

THE
DIVINE
GARDENER

SELWYN HUGHES

Illustrated by Brian Norwood

© CWR 1989

**CWR, 10 Brooklands Close,
Sunbury-on-Thames, Middx TW16 7DX**

NATIONAL DISTRIBUTORS

Australia: Christian Marketing Pty Ltd., PO Box 154, North Geelong,
Victoria 3215   Tel: (052) 786100

Canada: Canadian Christian Distributors Inc., PO Box 550, Virgil,
Ontario LOS 1TO   Tel: 416 641 0631

Eire: Merrion Press Ltd, 10 D'Olier Street, Dublin

Malaysia: Salvation Book Centre, (M) Sdn. Bhd., 23 Jalan SS2/64,
47300 Petaling Jaya, Selangor

New Zealand: CWR (NZ), PO Box 4108, Mount Maunganui
Tel: (075) 57412

Singapore: Alby Commercial Enterprises Pte Ltd., Garden Hotel,
14 Balmoral Road, Singapore 1025

Southern Africa: CWR (Southern Africa), PO Box 2020, Clareinch, 7740 RSA
Tel: (021) 712560

Typeset by Watermark, Watford

Printed & bound in Great Britain

ISBN 1–85345–030–8 Hardback
ISBN 1–85345–031–6 Limp
First published 1983 and reprinted in illustrated format 1989

INTRODUCTION

Many times during the years in which I have been a minister and a counsellor, I have had occasion to sit and talk with those who have been undergoing the painful process of "spiritual pruning". During such periods innumerable questions rise unbidden in the mind: What is God doing to me? Why does it hurt so much? When will it all end?

Spiritual pruning is an experience from which many shrink – myself included – but one that is essential if we are to become the people God wants us to be. Christian fruitfulness and productivity do not just happen: they are the result of careful planning and pruning. Our Lord put the truth in these gripping and arresting words: "I am the true Vine, and my Father is the Gardener. He lops off every branch that doesn't produce. And he prunes those branches that bear fruit for even larger crops" (John 15:1–2, The Living Bible).

The questions that people have put to me over the years in relation to this issue of spiritual pruning have clear scriptural answers. Many of these answers are delineated in this book. Someone has said: "He who knows the *why* of things can always cope with the *what*." It is my prayer that as you read these pages and learn the "why" of God's intentions, you will be able to give yourself more confidently to the purposes of the Divine Gardener.

Always remember, no matter how often the secateurs snip or how painful the pruning, your life is in good hands: it is your *Father* who is the Gardener.

Selwyn Hughes

THE DIVINE GARDENER ... WHO PRUNES

We are going to examine together the ways by which our heavenly Father – the Divine Gardener – goes about the task of pruning our lives in order to make them more fruitful and productive.

Let us be quite clear about one thing at the outset – there is no way to spiritual fruitfulness except through careful and relentless pruning. Conversion may be described as being grafted to Jesus Christ, the Vine, whereby His divine life begins to flow in us and through us. We are made partakers of the divine nature. The pruning process – cutting away the things that hinder or prevent our growth – provides for a continuous conversion in which we are converted from the irrelevant to the relevant, from being just busy to being fruitful. The Divine Gardener knows that it is possible to have the most luxuriant growth with no fruit. The useless non-fruit-bearing growth – the suckers that take life but give no fruit – must be cut away.

John 15:1–8

v. 2

In Japan, land is so scarce compared with the population, that everything must be cultivated to the maximum. In a hotel room in Tokyo some years ago, I saw an apple that was twice the size of an ordinary one. I said to myself, "This isn't an apple, it's a whole tree!" How do the Japanese achieve such amazing results? Mainly in two ways – fertilisation and pruning. And especially pruning. Every useless branch and every bit of unproductive growth is cut away so that everything is prepared for maximum fruitfulness. This is how it must be with us. If we are not able to give up, then we will not be able to give out.

It is vital that we see this process of pruning in

positive terms, for a negative attitude can greatly hinder the purposes of the Divine Gardener. The shears, or knife, which cut away at the non-fruit-bearing growth are held in the hands, not of an angel, nor, for that matter, an archangel, but in the hands of our loving heavenly Father. "I am the true vine," said Jesus, "and my *Father* is the gardener." Note the word 'Father'. Whatever needs to be done in your life, you are in good hands! Your *Father* is the Gardener. Psalm 103: 1–22 v. 13

Some people base their view of God, the Father, on the mental images of Him which flow through their minds. However, no man or woman has the resources within themselves to discover, unaided, the true and living God. Job asks: "Who by searching can find out Job 11:7 God?" (11:7). The answer is plain – no one! For what we find in our upward search for God is not God, but the projection of our thoughts into the heavens. We create God in the image of our imagination – and it is not a true image. India is probably the greatest illustration of the truth of this, for if God could have been discovered by human searching, then the philosophers of that land would have found Him. But have they? No. Through philosophy, they have come out with a God who is other than the God of the Bible.

Someone has facetiously described philosophy as "a blind man in a dark room looking for a black cat that isn't there". There is much truth in that jibe. Philosophical reasoning has searched in a dark universe for a philosophical God who isn't there. The God of the Bible can only be discovered by revelation. No one could ever imagine that the God of the universe would step out of heaven, come right down to earth, live in a human body and die on a Cross to redeem us. A love like that just doesn't exist – not in the category of philosophy. But seeing is believing. The Creator, knowing that we could never come to Him, came to us, and, through the revelation of the Bible, gives us the truth about Himself. And the truth is: He is not just omnipotent power but eternal Love.

1 John 4:1–15 v. 10

J. B. Phillips, in *Your God is too Small,* says that our concept of God is invariably founded upon a child's idea of his father. If he is fortunate enough to have had a kind, indulgent and considerate father, then, when he becomes a Christian, he tends to project that same image on to God. But if the child has a stern, punitive parent, of whom he lives in dread, the chances are that His Father in heaven will appear to him as a fearful being. Some outgrow such a misconception, and are

able to differentiate between the early 'fearful' idea and the later mature conception. But many don't. They carry a 'parental hangover' into their Christian life and *endure* rather than *enjoy* it because they are never quite sure that God has their highest interests at heart.

I wonder, is someone reading this who pictures God as tyrannical, judgmental, punitive, or just plain disinterested? Ask yourself: where did I get this picture of the Almighty? Not from the Scriptures. Decide now to leave behind all misconceptions, and discover the true God – the God of the Bible.

Luke 11:1–13
v. 13

How does the Bible convey to us a clear picture of God's heart and character? Well, it is not just the Book, wonderful though it is, but what the Book says about God's self-revelation in the person of His Son. You see, if God gave us a book containing the most intimate details of His heart, it would never have enabled us to know Him as He really is. We may catch glimpses of Him in the words He utters, but the only way God can be seen as He really is, is in the Incarnate life of His Son. There was, and is, no other way for God to reveal Himself, in understandable terms, except through a human life. He has to show His character where your character and mine are wrought out, namely in the stream of human history. So Jesus makes 'known' the character of God in the only possible way His character can be made known, namely through another character – His own.

John 1:1–18
v. 18

We have seen that before we can entrust ourselves to the pruning shears of the Divine Gardener, we must have absolute confidence in His abilities and character. Jesus, knowing the fears and uncertainties that linger in the human heart, went to great lengths to assure us that God's care for us runs down to the tiniest and most insignificant details. On one occasion, He took up the most extravagant metaphor He could find: *"The very hairs of your head are numbered"* (Matt. 10:30). Jesus' own untroubled spirit arose, I believe, from the fact that He had complete confidence that His Father's purposes were loving, wise and good. We see this in the last testing hours of His life. After His agony in the Garden of Gethsemane, when He is arrested, He declares, "Shall I not drink the cup *the Father has given me?"* Can you see what He is saying? The cup which He had been given to drink was full of bitterness, but He found solace in the fact that *the cup was in His Father's hands.* And so, my friend, must you.

Matthew
10:30

John 18:1–14
v. 11

PRUNING ... BY THE WORD

God prunes through His Word. Have you ever found
yourself reading the Scriptures when suddenly a verse
seems to leap out at you, fasten itself to your conscience
and plead with you to put something right in your life
that you know to be wrong? That was God at work,
pruning your life through His Word.

Hebrews
4:12–16
v. 12

In order for the Divine Gardener to prune us through
the Word, we must soak ourselves in that Word. As
Emily Dickinson put it:

> *"He ate and drank the precious words,*
> *His spirit grew robust ...*
> *He danced along the dingy days,*
> *And this bequest of wings*
> *Was but a book. What liberty*
> *A loosened spirit brings!"*

Indeed, what 'liberty' it brings if we expose our beings to
the Book, and give God the opportunity He desires to
prune away the suckers that take life, but give no fruit. I
believe with all my heart that the *chief* method by which
God desires to prune our lives is through His Word
contained in the Scriptures. The Bible is eminently suit-
able for this, because it is both searching and sensitive.

2 Timothy
3:10–17
v. 16

People often ask: Doesn't an emphasis on reading the
Bible *daily* bring Christians into a state of bondage and
legalism? Yes, it can, but with the right approach it need
not necessarily be so.

Romans
8:15

My own view is this – it is of immense spiritual benefit
to spend some time daily in the Bible, but we must be
careful not to think that if we miss out on reading a
portion of the Scriptures each day, God might push us

under a bus. Try to read the Word of God daily, but if for some reason, such as tiredness, sickness or a period of unusual pressure, you are not able to do so, don't be too hard on yourself, but return to a regular schedule as soon as you can. The goal in every Christian life ought to be that of spending some time every day in the Bible.

John 5:31–47
v. 39

None who seek to be conformed to the image of Christ can afford to neglect the Book. This doesn't mean, of course, that the only reason we ought to read the Bible is so that God can have an opportunity to knock us into shape. I doubt whether I would be motivated to open the Scriptures daily if I thought that every time I did so God would reprimand me. Of course, if my life was way out of line, then God would be justified in doing this, but *normally* God's way of ministering to us is to mix His blessings and speak through His Word right into the area of our current need. One day our greatest need might be for comfort; and so He says: "My grace is sufficient for you" (2 Cor. 12:9). Or it might be counsel. Then He says: "This is the way, walk ye in it" (Isa. 30:21). When our greatest need is reproof, then, of course, He speaks with the same authority and love.

2 Corinthians 12:9

Isaiah 30:21

Because our needs are so varied, that is why we should spend time with the *Bible* and not with substitutes. "Promise boxes" or booklets that contain selected verses dealing only with comfort, may be useful as sweetmeats, but they must never become the whole meal. If God is to develop our lives through Scripture, then we must take care to read as much of it as possible. As far as the Bible is concerned, God can develop most those who read it most.

CLEANSED ... BY THE WORD

After Jesus had been with His disciples for nearly three years, during which time they had watched Him and caught His ideas and His spirit, He turned to them and said: "You are already clean because of the word I have spoken to you" (John 15:3).

John 15:3

What was this 'Word' that made them clean? Why did He use 'Word' instead of 'words'? The reason could be that His words gathered themselves into such a living body of truth and insight, into such unity and oneness, that they were no longer words – they were 'the Word'. Over the period of time Christ spent with His disciples, His 'Word' had been at work in their lives, cleansing, purifying and pruning. When the disciples first joined Christ, they had some pretty strange ideas about God and about life. But gradually, being exposed to the Word, their ideas were cleansed and purified.

Ephesians 5:21–33 v. 26

Jesus (as we saw) cleansed their ideas about God. He got them to see that the Almighty was not an autocratic, irresponsible despot but a Father and a Friend. He not only cleansed their ideas about God, but He cleansed their ideas about the Kingdom of God. The Kingdom of God was, to the Jewish mind, a setting up of a power base from which God would rule with strength and force. Jesus showed them that the rule of God would not be by the force of might, but by the force of love.

He also cleansed their ideas about prayer. When they first came to Him, they obviously thought of prayer as getting something out of God, but they came to see that it was God getting something out of them. Through His Word, Jesus cleansed their total conception of life. And

as we, His 20th century disciples, heed His Word, the same thing will happen to us.

Jesus also *cleansed the family.* The home was the one and only institution He defended. But He not only defended it – He cleansed it. He cleansed it from polygamy on the one side and polyandry on the other, and took His disciples back to the original purpose of God in the Garden of Eden – of one man and one woman in equal partnership until parted by death (Matt. 19:5–6).

Matthew 19:5–6

He cleansed the idea of greatness. It was no longer to be seen as the possession of wealth or as having power over the lives of men. The greatest of all was to be the servant of all (Matt. 23:11).

Matthew 23:11

He cleansed religion. Jesus made Himself the definition of religion. He said, "I am the way – and the truth and the life. No one comes to the Father except through me" (John 14:6). To be religious, in the true sense of the word, is to be one of Christ's committed followers. His definition forever cleanses the mind from unworthy and lesser conceptions. A man objected, when in a meeting a minister said that religion was to be Christlike, and said, "But don't you shield unworthy religion behind your definition when you give such a definition of religion?" "No," said the minister, "I do not shield it, I cleanse it." When we have looked into the face of Jesus Christ, we can no longer think of religion except in terms of His wondrous life.

John 14:6

But Jesus went further and cleansed love. He found it as lust and left it as love. The love of which He spoke can be between those of the same sex, as well as those of the opposite sex, between the married or unmarried – and it is without lust (John 15:12–13). What a cleansing!

John 15:12–13

PREPARING TO BE PRUNED

Having seen how God uses His Word in the pruning process, we must ask ourselves: what steps do we take to get the best out of our daily reading of the Scriptures?

1. *Relax.* You are receptive only when you are relaxed. Nothing can be inscribed on a tense conscious mind.

Psalm
119:9–24
v. 18

2. *Recall.* Ask these questions as you read a passage: Who is writing? What is the purpose? How does it apply to me? How shall I put it into practice? When do I begin?

3. *Rehearse.* If you find a verse or a thought from the Word that speaks to your condition roll it over in your mind. Do as Spurgeon once suggested to his students. Take a choice portion of God's Word as you would a sweet – put it on the tip of your spiritual tongue and suck every precious drop of flavour from it!

4. *Retain.* If a verse or a part of a verse speaks to you decide to retain it by committing it to memory. When Jesus was pressed by temptation in the wilderness, He answered in the words of Scripture. The words had become part of Him, and in the crisis they passed from the stage of assimilation to that of advantage.

5. *Rejoice.* In reading the Word remember that the purpose of the Bible is to take you by the hand and lead you to the Word, which is Christ. So as you read, look for Him, and when you find Him – rejoice.

6. *Realign.* A quaint Negro preacher used to pray, "Prop us up, Lord, on our leaning side." The problems of life often cause us to get out of alignment with God's purpose for our existence, so as you read God's Word keep realigning your life with His life.

7. *Release.* When something grips you from the Word, pass it on to someone that very day. The repetition will help you retain it and might also lighten the path of the other person.

PRUNED ... BY THE SPIRIT

Another way in which the Divine Gardener goes about the task of pruning our lives for greater fruitfulness and effectiveness is that *He prunes through the Holy Spirit.* John 16:1–15

The Holy Spirit is referred to in various terms in the New Testament, one of which is the term 'paraclete'. The word 'paraclete' comes from two simple Greek words: *para,* which means 'alongside' and *kaleo,* which means v. 13 'to call' or 'to summon'. Can you see the picture? The Holy Spirit is the one who comes alongside us to help us in time of need, not least to plead and remonstrate with us whenever we are tempted to sin. One hymnist, when contemplating this aspect of the Holy Spirit's work, put it like this:

> *"O plead the truth and make reply*
> *To every argument of sin."*

The arguments of sin? What does that mean? One argument that sin advances is that moral violations don't really matter. Its voice cries out in the soul, "It isn't important – let yourself off lightly." But sin *does* matter. The Bible says plainly that "the wages of sin is Romans 6:23 death" (Rom.6:23). Where would you and I be right now in our Christian life if the blessed Paraclete had not come alongside us the moment we were seduced by sin, and 'pleaded the truth' with authority and conviction? He came and showed us that the first thing to do was to recognise the sin *as* sin, to repent of the wrong we had done, claim forgiveness from God, and hate the evil for the loathsome thing it was. I say again: if in the moment of overwhelming temptation He had left us without a word – where would we be?

Another 'argument' which sin advances is that of

rationalisation. To rationalise something is to make excuses for it, and sin is an expert at attempting to justify itself. Do you know anything about this? Something tells me that you do. Look at how it worked in the life of David, then you might be more ready to spot it in your own soul. David wanted the wife of one of his officers. While the officer was away on active service with his army, David seduced the woman. Then, fearing the consequences, he 'arranged' the death of her husband, adding the sin of murder to that of adultery and lust (2 Sam. 11).

2 Samuel 11

How did David, "the man after God's own heart", ever get into such a situation? He did it by rationalising. A sinful thought entered his mind, and instead of blasting it with prayer, he fed his imagination upon it. Once the sinful thought was entertained, it proceeded to upset his

moral compass. He made excuses for his immorality, and, as far as the death of Uriah was concerned, persuaded himself that gallant soldiers do fall to their death on the field of battle. He was, however, a victim of the arguments of sin. He rationalised his problem, and made excuses for himself. His mind became so blunted against reality that God had to use Nathan's barbed parable to get through to him.

2 Samuel
12:1–14

Another way by which sin seeks to enter our lives, and get past our guard, is through the use of euphemisms – calling a deadly or serious issue by a less offensive name. It calls a lie a 'fib', and stealing, 'scrounging'. It calls living a loose sexual life, 'love'. It calls the avoiding of responsibility, 'being smart'. It calls drunkenness, 'alcoholism'. It calls practising homosexuals, 'male lovers'.

A minister tells of a joint meeting of doctors, psychiatrists and ministers he once attended in a town in the north of England. The purpose of the meeting was to think through ways in which the various professions could work together. There was a great deal of talk about pre-marital and extra-marital sexual relationships. The minister said, "I knew, of course, what they were meaning by all that, but there was one old rural parson there who was confused by the terms, and couldn't keep up with the conversation. Finally he said, 'Pre-marital and extra-marital sexual relationships? Do you mean fornication and adultery?' Those plain, but Biblical, words came like a bombshell to that highly-trained and sophisticated group of men.

We live in an age, which, as you well know, likes to gloss things over with less challenging names, and that is one way in which society greases the path to sin. The

Holy Spirit, however, works in the hearts of those who are His, encouraging them to see sin for the ugly thing it is, and to stubbornly refuse to change the labels. A deadly thing is not made innocuous by a less distasteful name. Leukaemia is still leukaemia even when you call it 'a problem in the blood'.

Romans 8:1–11 v. 5

Another 'argument' of sin is: *everybody does it.* I recently came across a report of a certain denomination in Scandinavia, where the young people were engaged in a great deal of sexual permissiveness. Some of the leaders of the denomination argued that the clear principles of Scripture ought to be expounded so that the young people might have some moral guidelines. Others said, "Well, most young people sleep around these days – it's part of the 20th century lifestyle – so let's not try to stamp it out, but encourage them to be

faithful to one partner, and not to become promiscuous in their love-making." Despite some objections, the matter was finally put to the vote and carried.

How sad that a so-called Christian denomination can settle a moral issue such as this by popular vote rather than by the clear standards of Scripture. Oh, how desperately we need the cleansing flow of the Holy Spirit to flood our lives and reinforce our moral convictions. In Christ's name, I plead with you, don't fall for the argument that says "everybody does it": the matter of sin must be seen in a new light.

Cast your eyes on 1 Corinthians 10:13. What does it say? Surely that settles the issue once and for all. No, I am not unmindful of the struggles and temptations of the flesh, neither am I unaware of the strong forces that surge within us, clamouring for expression; but I have to be faithful to Scripture, and say with equal emphasis that all the resources of heaven are engaged against sin. It is false reasoning to excuse sin on the grounds that everybody does it. God promises a way of escape.

1 Corinthians 10:1–13

The Holy Spirit refutes all these 'arguments' for sin and pleads for truth and righteousness in our lives. I say again: where would you and I have been but for that blessed Paraclete? If, at our first encounter with sin; if, as soon as we were seduced in our hearts by desire; if, when our vagrant nature clamoured for sinful expression; if He had left us without a word ... where would we have been? How grateful we ought to be that the Divine Gardener has given us the Holy Spirit to be *always* present in our lives, so that when evil desires begin to plead the arguments of sin, there is another voice that rises in the court of our soul, pleading for *holy* things.

John 14:1–21 vv. 16–17

Some years ago at the Sheffield Quarter Sessions a

case was held up because a judge complained that he could not 'see' a barrister in court. The barrister was there, but he was not wearing his wig and gown. According to English law, the judge can only see an advocate when he is properly attired. There was a prisoner in the dock, and a barrister ready to plead his cause, but his plea could not be given because, according to the courts, he was 'invisible'. There was no one to plead for the prisoner. No one to say, "He has learned his lesson, he will not fall so easily again."

I am bold enough to say that in the lives of those of you who belong to Jesus Christ, the Holy Spirit will always be visible. He is always ready to stand up in the courtroom of your soul to plead the truth and make reply to every argument of sin. So take heart – He is *always* there.

PRUNED ... BY PRAYER

God has many pruning knives, and it will help us in our Christian life if we know them all. Let us look at how *God prunes our lives through prayer.* Acts 9:10–18

One of my favourite definitions of prayer is the one used by Kagawa, the Japanese Christian leader, who said that "prayer is *revision*". He went on to explain what he meant in these impressive words: "A revised version of your life is published every time you pray, really pray. For in the silence before Him, you bring more and more areas of your life under His control, more and more powers are put at His disposal, more and more channels

of receptivity are opened up and more and more alignments of our wills are made to the will of God."

One of the reasons why God calls us to prayer is because He knows that much of our lives become overgrown with suckers that sap our strength, bear no fruit themselves and keep us from bearing fruit. Suckers (like many of the things that clutter our lives) are not bad in themselves: they simply draw from us the strength that should go into fruit-bearing. How many of us, I wonder, are busy doing nothing! We rush here and there, but achieve little. We are like the Texan of whom it was said that "he jumped on his horse and went off in all directions". When we get down before God in prayer,

and take time to *listen* to what He has to say to us, He brings the important to the centre of consciousness and pushes the unimportant to the edge. Therefore, in prayer, that is *listening* prayer, God prunes our purposes and our persons.

People often say to me, "How are you able to keep on constantly writing *Every Day with Jesus,* preparing the seminars, and the other things in which you are involved?" I have one simple answer – *prayer.* I do not wish to present myself as an expert in prayer (God knows how often I grieve before Him because I do not pray as long or as often as I ought), but I have found that the more I pray, the more effectively and quickly I can accomplish my tasks. Those who say they are too busy to pray are fooling themselves. If they prayed, then God would come to them and help them prune their lives for greater fruitfulness and effectiveness.

Permit me to share with you some of the things I have learned through prayer in relation to the best use of time:

(1) In prayer, God prunes our lives so that we achieve His highest purposes. Many of us live lives that are overgrown and cluttered up with the unimportant. We are busy doing nothing. The more we pray, the more God is able to separate the irrelevant from the relevant, and show us the things upon which we ought to concentrate. Just before Jesus suffered upon the Cross, He said "I have brought you glory on earth by completing the work *you* gave me to do" (John 17:4). John 17:4 There were many things Jesus could have done, which would have been helpful and beneficial to the people of His day, but because He had a list of priorities, which had been worked out in prayer, He kept to them, and Luke 2:41–52 achieved, not just a good purpose, but God's purpose. v. 49

And the result? Mission accomplished.

We must not see this pruning through legalistic spectacles, however, and view God as a strict schoolmaster, bending over us and demanding that we make use of every minute of our time. We need time to relax, unwind, and forget our responsibilities. Jesus enjoyed such times. "Come with me," He once said to His disciples, "and get some rest" (Mark 6:31). I have found that the more I pray, the more effectively and quickly I can fulfil my tasks – therefore, the more time I have for relaxation. Prayer helps us to see clearly the things God wants us to do, and we have all the time we need to perform *His* tasks.

Mark 6:31

(2) Another thing I have learned through prayer is how to use the two letters of the alphabet – N and O – 'No'! In the early years of my life, I was a people-pleaser. I tended to take on more tasks than were good for me, because I hated to disappoint anyone. Prayer pruned me of the desire to please people, and gave me an overwhelming desire to please God. Now, whenever I am asked to speak at a certain meeting or conference, I take the matter to the Lord. If He gives me permission, I say 'Yes', but if I do not get His mind on the matter, then I say 'No'. Once I used to accept every invitation, and I almost broke down under what someone has called the "burden of busyness".

1 John 2:7–17
v. 17

Do you find it easy to say 'No'? Thousands of Christians are unable to do so. They become easy prey for those in the Church who like to manipulate people into doing what they think they should do. If you are one of those people who can't say 'No', then you need to ask yourself: who has my first allegiance – God, or others?

(3) The importance of spare minutes. Talk to anyone who is involved in doing great work for God (or, for that matter, anyone involved in the running of a successful business), and you will probably find that that person is a 'minute-minder'. Productive people know how to use those spare minutes that invariably crop up in even the busiest days. This explains why busy people, given additional jobs, get them done.

Proper use of idle moments reveals a positive outlook on life. Those who use spare minutes to turn over critical thoughts, or rehash lost battles, come out with unhealthy attitudes, but the person who converts spare minutes into constructive thinking will make a mark on

Colossians 4:2–6
v. 5

the world. Strauss wrote one of his famous waltzes on the back of a menu while waiting for his meal in a Viennese restaurant. Harriet Beecher Stowe gripped a pencil between her teeth while kneading dough, so that, in between times, she could write snatches of "Uncle Tom's Cabin". George Müller used to pray while he shaved every morning. What does your mind do when it has nothing to do? The answer to that will determine the kind of person you are. Some people allow their minds to dwell upon all kinds of fantasies, old arguments or past failures.

When the architect of a European cathedral came to insert the stained-glass windows, he found that he was

one window short. Frantically he wondered what could be done. His assistant solved the problem. Collecting the fragments of glass which had been set aside, he finally produced a window that harmonised with the others. Some said it was the most beautiful of all! If much of life is overgrown with the unimportant and the irrelevant, then any time we spend with God in prayer, so that He can prune us for greater fruitfulness, is time well spent.

(4) The fourth lesson God wants to teach us in this respect is the value of time. We must not become obsessive about it, but our lives will be lived with greater effectiveness for God if we learn to value the minutes, the hours and the days the Almighty gives us. This

Ephesians
5:8–20

vv. 15–16

resolve must become an integral part of our daily thinking: "Time is valuable. While I must not become obsessive about it, I must watch carefully the minutes that flow through my hands, and dedicate myself to spending my time as wisely as possible to the glory of God."

The Christian who wants to make the best use of his time must have a keen awareness of its value. Time should be regarded with great importance, for it is God-given. Though others may have more talents, we all have the same amount of time. God gives it to all, equally. Time cannot be bought, no matter how rich you are. And no matter how poor, you won't receive less. The

Archbishop of Canterbury has no more time than you and me. Every one of us has 60 minutes to the hour, 24 hours to the day and seven days per week. However, perhaps the greatest reason why time should not be wasted is because it is irrevocable. I noticed this ad. in the newspaper: "Lost, yesterday, somewhere between sunrise and sunset, two golden hours, each set with sixty diamond minutes. No reward, they are gone forever." Someone has said: "Yesterday is a cancelled cheque. Tomorrow is a promissory note. Today is the only cash you have. Spend it wisely."

We have one more lesson to learn about how God prunes our time through prayer: (5) Budget your time.

The best way to use money is by budgeting. It is the same with time. "When you budget your time," says Dr Edward Hakes, an expert on time-management, "you discover that you don't have to 'buy' everything ... you 'buy' with time only those activities worth 'buying'. Without some attempt to budget, you waste time, and 'buy' activities not worth the expenditure." Just as we have a financial budget, so we should have a time budget for the tasks of the immediate future. The people who make a schedule and keep revising it, weighing every item, are the people who move on that straight line: the shortest distance between two points. I know that I would never get done what has to be done were it not for a daily budget of my time.

A motto I saw on someone's desk, although humorous, has a good deal of sense. "Think! Maybe you can dodge some work!" It's not just funny – it's true. Thinking is the greatest time-saving activity. A few minutes at the start of each day, prayerfully and carefully planning the programme for the day ahead, is the most productive way I know of getting the best out of each day. One needs to know what is important, what is less important and what is trivial. The most difficult decisions should be made in the morning while the mind is fresh. Some advocate making out a schedule the night before. This way one can start right the next morning. If we plan each day with God, then we won't need to spend so much time fretfully re-examining our decisions. After all, time is not ours, but His.

2 Corinthians 5:11–21

v. 15

PRUNED ... THROUGH THE CHURCH

We move on now to examine yet another way by which
God prunes our lives for greater fruitfulness and
effectiveness. *God prunes through the Church.* The
ministries that function in Christ's Church are
designed, not only for our encouragement and
edification, but for our spiritual correction as well.

Looking back over my life, I am filled with gratitude to
God for the way He has prodded me into usefulness, not
only through His Word or directly by His Spirit, but also
through the ministries which He has placed in His Body,
the Church. Take first the ministry of teaching and
preaching. How many times have you listened to a

Ephesians
4:1–13
v. 11

preacher or Christian teacher and realised that what he was saying was a direct word from God to yourself? I remember as a youth walking into a church in Merthyr Tydfil where Idris Davies was preaching. I was somewhat cold in my heart toward the Lord at that time, but as soon as he began to speak, I sensed that this was God's message direct to my heart. I tried to get out of my seat, but felt as if invisible cords bound me to it. I wriggled, I squirmed, I resisted, I argued, but God's Word penetrated to the depth of my heart like a rapier. That night, I surrendered, not just a part, but the whole of my being to Jesus Christ. When I spoke to others later, they seemed to regard the sermon as nothing out of the ordinary, but for me it was like receiving a telegram

direct from heaven. I said to a friend of mine on the way out, "I've had my insides sand-papered here today."

Have you had a similar experience? Have you sat in church, listened to a preacher, and known that this was a challenge straight from God to your heart? Then you will know what I mean when I say God prunes through preaching.

He also prunes through the small fellowship group. Acts 2:42–47 v. 42 For many years I lived without a disciplined group correction. My life was overgrown with a lot of useless things. However, when I joined a disciplined group, the pruning process began. I have said before that every Christian needs to be involved in a small group of loving, caring believers, where the true *"koinonia"* can be developed. *Koinonia* is the Greek word for fellowship: the kind of fellowship which functions under the constraint of love and truth. Notice I say love *and* truth. Some Christians are good at speaking the truth, but bad at loving. Others are good at loving, but hesitate to speak the truth, or the whole truth. How impoverished we are in the 20th century Church because we do not cultivate such groups. There are notable exceptions, of course, but they are few and far between.

In one group to which I belonged, a person said very gently and lovingly, "I notice that whenever someone has a problem, you seem to want to come right in with the answer. Is it possible that perhaps sometimes God might want to use someone else to give an answer?" I was corrected – and in this case by someone who had not been a Christian for more than a year. Following that group encounter, I have learned to hold back, to see whether someone else might have the answer, before sharing my own thoughts or views on an issue. It was a

necessary pruning. The small fellowship group, if properly constructed and supervised, is one of the most effective pruning processes in the world.

In many cities in the USA (and now beginning in Great Britain and parts of Europe), Christians are meeting in small groups which are called Ashrams. The word, taken from India, consists of *a* (from) and *shram* (work), and means a cessation of work: a place where one retires for spiritual help and discipline. I think it sad when people have to join such groups because their own

church does not cultivate the true koinonia. Fortunately there are signs that the Church is recognising the need for small fellowship groups, not just groups for prayer or Bible study, but groups where people are free to share their deepest needs.

"I'm afraid to be a part of a group where people share on a deep level," said one woman to a friend of mine. When he asked why, she replied, "I'm not afraid of sharing myself, but I am afraid of criticism." However, as you know, there is a world of difference between

destructive and constructive criticism. Christian criticism is always constructive – or else it isn't Christian. The woman eventually joined a sharing group, and is growing by leaps and bounds.

1 John
4:7–21
v. 11

It goes without saying, of course, that the ministries in the Church function in other ways beside correction, but as this is the aspect we are discussing, we shall look at them from that point of view.

Another ministry God uses to prune us is that of personal counselling. There are those in every community of God's people who are gifted by Him for the work of individual counselling. Perhaps you may be one. If you find yourself motivated to search out answers for people's problems, and long to help them unravel their spiritual and psychological difficulties, the chances are it is because the gift is working within you.

Here again, I feel the Church is failing in its mission because it doesn't seem able to help its members discover and develop their basic spiritual gifts. One of the greatest needs in the Church at this time is for its leaders (pastors, elders, deacons) to show people how to discover and exercise their basic gifts. If this was done, then I am convinced that there would be many who would discover within them the gift of counselling, and, with guidance and instruction, could use that gift to restore struggling and bound-up Christians to fuller and more productive lives. If Christians were to unwrap their gifts, particularly the gift of counselling, and, with God's help, assist struggling believers toward greater fruitfulness and effectiveness, then we would convey to the world, not just by our lips, but also by our lives, that Christ is truly all-sufficient.

Romans
12:3–8

PRUNED ... THROUGH THE EUCHARIST

God also works to prune us for greater fruitfulness
through the Eucharist or Holy Communion. The 1 Corinthians
Communion service has many wonderful aspects, not 11:17–34
the least being that of self-examination. "A man ought to
examine himself," says the apostle, "before he eats of the v. 28
bread and drinks of the cup."

We ask ourselves: why does God, speaking through
the apostle Paul, command us to examine ourselves
before we take the bread and wine? Where better? It is at
the foot of the Cross that we discover the mainspring of
all Christian action. Some press on to perfection and

self-improvement out of a desire to earn God's approval. They long to hear the words, "Well done, good and faithful servant." Sometimes there is a tinge of self-centredness in such a desire. We like to feel that we have done something to *deserve* His love.

I have said often that the mainspring of any Christian action, be it caring, evangelism or self-discipline, should not be on the basis of attempting to earn His love, but on the basis that we are already loved. In bidding us come to the Communion Table to examine ourselves, God wants us to see how much He loves us so that love, not fear, can be the challenge that brings about change. You see, if you try to love God without first realising how

much He loves you, then all attempts at self-improvement and self-discipline will be mechanical. In the light of His love for us at Calvary, as vividly dramatised through the bread and the wine, we are fortified to let go of all that is unlike Him, and to let Him love us into greater Christlikeness. John captured the thought most effectively when he said, "We love...*because*" (1 John 4:19).

1 John 4:19

Now we must consider the matter of church discipline. A letter I received recently from a minister says, "I have in my church a member who is involved in a serious moral sin. He does not try to hide it. What can I do? If I make an issue of it, I know I will split my church." I can sympathise with this minister's predicament. After all, who wants to kill a church?

The problem of church discipline is a thorny one, but it is one the Church must take up, nevertheless. God is eager and ready to forgive anyone who is repentant and willing to give up their sin, but when sinful behaviour continues in the life of a Christian, then the Church must obey the Word of Christ and institute disciplinary action. People fear that discipline will divide and destroy the Church. Actually the opposite is true. Wise Biblical discipline will unite the Church, revive its spirit and produce solid growth. My words might sound strong, and, in some quarters, may be resisted, but those churches who refuse to institute proper disciplinary measures are in danger of having Christ withdraw His presence from them.

Can Christ leave a local church? He left the Laodicean church. Outwardly they got along so well without Him, they never even missed Him. They had forgotten their dependence and their loyalty to Him. So He delivered

Revelation 3:14–22

v. 16

the church over to judgment. Disgusted, He spat them out of His mouth. There is no eternal security for a local church. The Lord doesn't have to come just because we invoke His Name. He knows when He is no longer in charge, and when He sees it to be so, He leaves.

Church discipline has two principal purposes. First, it preserves the character of the Church. Second, it saves the soul of the offender. At one time, Paul called for the excommunication of an unrepentant immoral believer "so that the sinful nature may be destroyed and his spirit saved on the day of the Lord" (1 Cor. 5:5, NIV). Discipline saves a believer by restoring him to

1 Corinthians 5:5

obedience. Obedience, believe me, is the only place of safety for a Christian. Salvation has been described as "escaping from the kingdom of Satan, and finding protection under the gracious rule of Christ". Disobedience, here, means much more than a temporary lapse – it means a continued, wilful persistence in sin.

Where do we start? Exactly what sins call for discipline? Do we discipline people who, as we say, *have* to get married? Or what about people who get caught exceeding the speed limit? Or, again, what about someone who has been convicted of crime? The issue is

Galatians 6:1

not what sin a Christian has committed, but whether he
has repented. Is he walking with God now? Discipline
aims to produce repentance and restore fellowship.
Under the guidance of the Holy Spirit, the Church must
give whatever discipline is required to accomplish these
objectives.

2 Corinthians
2:5–11

In eighteen years of pastoral ministry, only once, on
behalf of a church, did I excommunicate a member. He
went out bitter and rebellious, but within two years he
came back changed and repentant. In an acceptance
meeting, he said, "I'm glad you loved me enough to take
that final action." When a church fails to discipline, it
loses its soul. That is why the church must discipline –
or die.

PRUNED ... BY AUTHORITY

Another aspect of how the Divine Gardener prunes our lives for greater fruitfulness is *through the authorities He places over us.* I'm amazed at the number of Christians I meet who fail to see that the principle of authority is not something thought up by autocratically-minded individuals, who delight in lording it over others, but is something which the Creator established when He designed the universe. I like the way J.B.Phillips translates verse 2 of Romans 13: "To oppose authority then is to oppose God, and such opposition is bound to be punished."

Romans 13:1–7
v. 2

The wave of anti-authority sweeping the world at the moment is yet another evidence of mankind's stubborn refusal to bring their lives in line with the design which God has set for them. This general attitude of anti-authority is, I fear, in danger of infiltrating the ranks of those who are followers of the Lord Jesus Christ.

Some time ago I had occasion to speak to a Christian who told me that he was thinking of changing his job because he couldn't stand the personality of the man who was over him. I said, "Have you considered that God may want to use the irritating characteristics of your boss as a kind of hammer and chisel to chip away at the rough spots in your personality?" He admitted that he had never considered it in that way, but he promised to give the matter some further thought. He wrote to me later to say that the concept of seeing his boss as God's hammer and chisel transformed his attitudes towards God, towards his work and towards himself. God prunes through many things, not the least the authority He places over us.

That the age through which we are passing is one of anti-authority is due partly to Satan's influence in human affairs, for it is part of his strategy to persuade men that the violation of divine principles is in their best interest. There is good reason to believe that Satan seeks to bring about deception in the area of authority more than in any other. His very spirit of rebellion was the cause of his own downfall, and he attempts today to deceive even God's children with plausible arguments that are opposed to God's order and design.

Isaiah 14:12–23
vv. 13–14

A careful examination of Scripture shows that the principle of authority comes into operation at all stages of our development. We first begin to understand

authority through the disciplines of home and family life (Eph. 6:1–4). Later, we come in contact with it when we start school, and later still when we take up employment (Col. 3:22–25). God has established in society a structure of authority by which men and women can live peaceably and in harmony with one another (Rom.13:1–2). Once we become Christians, we become members of the Christian Church, where there is also a clear line of authority (Eph. 4:11–12). Almost every day of our lives we find ourselves in situations and circumstances which bring us directly under someone's authority, and unless we see that God wants to use this authority to bring His purposes to pass in our lives, then

Ephesians 6:1–4

Colossians 3:22–25

Romans 13:1–2

Ephesians 4:11–12

we will miss out on one of life's greatest character-building processes.

One of the most freeing insights of Scripture is the fact that God is the highest authority in the universe, and works through all lesser authorities to prune our lives and develop our effectiveness. It is 'freeing' because, once we discover it and grasp it, we have the insight we need to cope with any pressure that is put on us by those who are in authority over us. We know, as Jesus said to Pilate, "You have no power over me that was not given to you from above" (John 19:11).

John 19:11

Are you under pressure at the moment from the authority over you at work, at school, at home, or at church? Is it hard to take? Then instead of focusing on

the authority that is immediately over you, lift your gaze higher to the highest authority of all – God. Ask yourself: is God allowing this pressure because He sees in me a character deficiency which He wants to correct? Is He permitting, or even influencing, the person who is over me to come down upon me more heavily than usual because He wants to bring about important changes in me?

Once we see that the hand of God may be at work, and expressed through the attitudes and actions of those in authority over us, we begin to learn something of how such pressure can, in the Almighty's purposes, work for good in our lives. Any failure on our part to observe how God works through the authority over us can hinder His

Philippians
2:1–13
v. 13

purposes for us and prevent us from entering into all that He plans for us. The most important thing we can discover, when under pressure from authority, is not how to get away from it, but to ask God what lesson He may be trying to teach us in the circumstances. Once that lesson is learned, then God will see that the pressure is released.

Whenever I mention the subject of a right Christian attitude to authority in any meeting where questions are invited, someone usually asks: "The person over me is unfair, inconsistent and undeserving of respect. How can I obey someone I cannot respect?" My answer is this: a person in authority over us may have many character deficiencies. He may have a bad temper, use obscene language, be subject to moodiness, shout, rave or become abusive, but these deficiencies must not stop us from adopting an attitude of respect for the person's *position*, even if we find it difficult to respect that individual's personality. You see, when you respect a

person's *position* of authority, you are respecting God, for it was He who ordained authority in this universe. Once you see this, then you have in your hands the key to the development of the right attitude towards authority. It is more important for you to recognise that God is working through even the deficiencies of the one above you, to bring about improvements in your character, than it is for that person to act more kindly and considerately towards you.

Our Christian growth is often hindered by wrong attitudes, and suffers more from a wrong attitude toward authority than any other thing. One of the first lessons we must learn, therefore, is to respond as God wants us to respond, irrespective of whether the authority over us improves or not.

Colossians
3:12–25
v. 23

Romans 14:1–8
v. 7

Everyone is under authority (or should be), and the person who is a law unto himself is in an extremely dangerous position – morally and spiritually.

In the family, the child comes under the authority of its parents, the wife under the authority of her husband, and the husband under the authority of God. In the Church, God expects us to be under the authority of those whom He calls to leadership positions. In society, we are expected to be under the authority of the laws of the land, enforced by the police and the magistrates.

In the home, in the Church and in society, we must recognise that all legitimate authority is derived from God's authority. Once we see this, and live by it, then we bring our lives in line with the fundamental structure of the universe, and we are on our way to real living.

PRUNED ... UNDER ATTACK

God uses *the attacks of Satan* to advance our progress and develop our spiritual effectiveness. Moffatt translates John 14:31 like this: "His (Satan's) coming will only serve to let the world see that I love the Father and that I am acting as the Father ordered." Our Lord made even Satan serve! And when the Master has control of your life, He can do the same for you, and turn the attacks of Satan to your spiritual advantage.

John 14:25–31

The secret of Jesus' power, to turn Satan's coming to advantage, is contained in the words: "The Prince of this world is coming. He has no hold on me" (Moffatt). There was nothing in our Lord's personality through which Satan could gain an advantage – no sin, no self-pity, no bitterness, no self-centredness. So Christ was able to turn the efforts of Satan towards positive ends.

The same, of course, cannot be said of us, for we are sinners, albeit *saved* sinners, with a lot of sinfulness and self-centredness still resident in our natures. Despite this difficulty, however, God, Christ and the Holy Spirit are working hand in hand to help us overcome our sinful nature; and such is the skill and wisdom of the Trinity that they can use even the attacks of Satan to further those purposes. Do you feel as if you are being attacked by Satan at this moment? Are you conscious of being the victim of strange diabolical pressures? Then take heart. God has promised that He will not permit Satan to inflict upon you more than you are capable of bearing (1 Cor. 10:13). As you draw close to Him, He will make the attacks of Satan *serve*.

1 Corinthians 10:13

We can look at the apostle Paul under attack. There is

a wide difference of opinion amongst Christians as to what precisely was Paul's "thorn in the flesh". Some believe it to be a sickness, such as recurring malaria or failing eyesight. They deduce this from the description Paul gives – "thorn in the *flesh*". The phrase, or a similar phrase, however, is used several times in the Scriptures, and always refers to personalities, never to things or conditions (Num. 33:55, Josh. 23:13 & 2 Sam. 23:6). These statements refer to people who were going to be extremely hurtful to the nation of Israel.

It is most likely that Paul, being a student of the Old Testament Scriptures, would have used it in the same way. This argument is greatly strengthened by what he says: "There was given me a thorn in my flesh, a *messenger* of Satan, to torment me." The word 'messenger', here translated from the Greek 'aggelos',

2 Corinthians
12:1–10
v. 7

Numbers 33:55
Joshua 23:13
2 Samuel 23:6

always denotes a person, never an object. Paul's "thorn in the flesh" (so I believe) was an evil spirit specially commissioned by Satan to harass the apostle in his work and bring about his downfall and defeat.

Three times, Paul prayed that this "messenger of Satan" might be removed, but God permitted him to stay, and continue to harass the apostle. Why? Because the Almighty, who saw things from an eternal perspective, knew that Paul would be a greater servant, and a more effective witness, *with* the harassment than he would be without it. God matched the challenge, however, with a special supply of His unfailing grace, and in this way made Satan's coming *serve*.

We can see a similar victory in the life of the Old Testament patriarch – Job. First, let me say that I believe that Job was singled out by God to become a classic example of unconditional faith in God, and that today's Christians should not walk around wondering if at any moment God is going to allow Satan to invade their lives with all kinds of disasters and catastrophes.

Job, you notice, had a 'hedge' around him. What does it mean – a 'hedge'? God, I believe, has providentially established a boundary of spiritual protection around every human life, for if not, Satan's power, being what it is, would eliminate every child born into the world. The Almighty God, protective of the life He creates, ensures that Satan does not have an open door into human personality. If this were not so, there would be much greater chaos in human affairs than there is.

Some people may, through dabbling with the occult, or by consulting Satan in séances, break open that hedge. Then, of course, unless they repent and turn to Christ, they openly expose themselves to Satan and his

Job 1:1–22
v. 10

power. In Job's case, God took away the protective hedge from around His servant so that Satan could enter his life in a way not normally permitted, and inflict upon him the full extent of his strategies. Job, of course, came through victoriously, proving that it was possible for a man to serve God because he loved Him, and not for personal advantage. We need to keep in mind that Satan's attacks come under the strict supervision of the Almighty, and He permits only that which accords with His eternal purposes.

The question is often asked: why does God permit the devil to have such power? Why, for that matter, didn't God eliminate Lucifer as soon as he had sinned, and thus spare the universe from a good deal of chaos and suffering?

We can never fully answer that question because, quite simply, we are unable to see into the divine mind. However, I have no doubt myself that the answer is partly because God, knowing the end from the beginning, knew that He could turn all Satan's efforts to advantage; and this, at the end of the day, would justify the Almighty's decision. This answer, I know, does little for those who point out the terrible suffering that Satan's rebellion has brought into the universe, but I believe that even that, when viewed from the divine standpoint in eternity, will be seen as necessary to God's overall purposes.

Satan, therefore, has his uses. One such can be seen in our Lord's life when He was confronted by Satan in the wilderness. Although it is not in the nature of God to tempt, He allowed Satan to try to take advantage of Jesus after His forty-day fast in the wilderness, and so attempt to bring about His downfall. But watch what happens. Christ, in His weakened condition, triumphs over the devil's repeated temptations, and comes out of the wilderness in the "power of the Spirit". Notice, He went in *full* of the Holy Spirit (v.1), and came out in the *power* of the Spirit (v.14). What did Satan's attacks succeed in doing? They helped to turn mere fulness to power. Our Lord's spiritual tissues had been hardened in the struggle.

Luke 4:1–14

v. 1
v. 14

When we stay close to Christ, then our own battles with the devil will have the same effect – our spiritual tissues become hardened in the struggle. One of Wales' greatest theologians, Dr Cynddylan Jones, used to say that two things happen as we face Satan's attacks in the strength and power of Jesus Christ: (1) Our temptations move on to a higher plane, and (2) we outgrow many of them. When you examine the temptations of Jesus, you find that they were on a very high plane indeed. He did not struggle with lust and passion, but with the more subtle questions of how to bring in the Kingdom. "It is a compliment," says Cynddylan Jones, "when we are tempted on that level. It shows that we are growing spiritually." Here temptations become less gross and more subtle. The battle with things, like spiritual pride, takes the place of the battle with lust, greed, dishonesty and lies. Then there comes a time, through experience and conflict, when you outgrow many temptations of Satan.

Revelation
3:7–13
v. 10

A man I know, who held an important position in local government in Cardiff, was imprisoned for accepting a bribe. While in prison, he was converted, and when he came out, he worked his way back to a responsible position in society. He now has the respect of hundreds of people. He told me once, "I say this humbly, and in dependence on God, but I don't think I could ever again be tempted by bribery. My character automatically spurns it."

I have talked with many Christians over the years, some of whom have now gone on to glory, and I have noticed that those who appear to be immune from temptation, reveal, in private conversation, that their immunity was won through a series of spiritual battles. I know in my own life that temptations, which would at one time have shaken me to the very foundation of my being, now have little impact upon me. This is not true of all temptations, but it is true of most. I have, as one writer put it, "got into the habit of experiencing victory." I say this, of course, in utter dependence on the Holy Spirit, for I am fully conscious that in this life we never achieve full immunity from temptation. However, I find that, more and more, the unconscious effort takes over the functions of the conscious effort. To my delight and amazement, I find I am becoming fixed in goodness. Habit is now working for me where once it worked against me.

v. 57

Those of you reading these lines who are struggling with some strong and fierce temptations – take heart. God is permitting you to be engaged in a battle with Satan which will not deprive you but deepen you. In His strength and power, you will emerge from this conflict with a refinement and a poise that you never thought possible. The battle will serve to show you that it is "not by might, nor by power, but by my spirit, saith the Lord" (Zech. 4:6). You will rejoice, not in what you can do, but in what He can do within you.

Zechariah 4:6

PRUNED ... BY PUZZLES

Another method which the Divine Gardener uses in pruning and prodding us toward greater fruitfulness is *through perplexing events and difficult situations which He allows to come into our lives.* Some of these events and situations may have evil ingredients in them, but it must be clearly understood that although God sometimes uses evil, He does not purpose it or design it. The only reason God permitted evil in His universe was because He knew He could outwit it and turn it to good.

Romans 8:28–3!
v. 28

Romans 8:28, as translated in the Authorised Version – "All things work together for good to them that love God" – may give the impression that God is responsible for everything that happens to us, but a closer examination of that text shows differently. One of the best translations is that of the NIV, "And we know that in all things God works for the good of those who love him".

The slight difference in the wording is crucial. To say that "all things work together for good" is not the same as saying "we know that in all things God works for the good of those who love him". All things do not necessarily work together for good: they may work for evil. To say that "*in* all things God works for the good" endows those 'things' with purpose – a purpose for good to those who love Him. Things by themselves have no purpose unless we and God put a purpose in them. The 'things' may not be good, and may not themselves work together for good, but 'in' those things God places His purpose, and makes them contribute to His ends. He turns the evil into good if we co-operate with Him and love Him.

Many times, when Christians quote Romans 8:28,

they recite the first part of the verse, but for some reason seem reluctant to complete it. They say, "All things work together for good," but that is only half of the matter. The other part of the verse says, "to them that love God, to them who are the called according to his purpose." The verse needs to be completed in order to be fully understood. God is able to use everything that happens to us and make it contribute to His, and our good, but only when we love Him and co-operate with Him.

Why is our love and co-operation so necessary for God to further His purposes through the difficult events and situations that arise from time to time in our lives? The answer is found in a statement I have used hundreds of times and I make no apology for using it again. It contains a most powerful and life changing truth: *it is*

not so much what happens to us, but how we view it that is important. In other words, our inner attitudes determine the final results. God's ability to make a difficult or unpleasant situation work for good is limited by our capacity to love Him and co-operate with Him. If we love Him, we will trust Him, and if we trust Him, then we will rest assured that nothing that happens to us can successfully work against us. To triumph in adversity means that God is doing His part and you are doing yours.

1 John 4:7–21

v. 18

First, we need to realise that, although we are Christians, we are not exempt from the ordinary problems and difficulties that afflict humanity. If we insist that we ought to be exempt, then, when adversity strikes, we will go down like ninepins. If we say such

things as, "Why should this happen to me? I'm a Christian. God should treat me better," then we take the first step toward depression and disillusionment.

Someone might say, "What difference, then, does it make in being a Christian?" A Christian has (if he wishes to embrace it) a perspective on life that assures him that whatever happens can be used. Unfortunately, not all Christians see it in these terms, and instead of being sweetened by life's situations, they are soured by them. Paul the apostle had this perspective. He said: "If I am in distress, it is in the interests of your comfort" (2 Cor. 1:6, Moffatt). He made his distress contribute to other people's comfort. The distress was a pruning that made him more fruitful. A Sunday school teacher drew up a list of qualities that were characteristic of Christians.

2 Corinthians 1:6

She listed such things as love, forgiveness, gentleness, honesty, and so on. A little boy put up his hand and said, "Miss, you've missed out the most important." "What is that?" she asked. "Please miss, the way to take things on the chin." He was right! When life hits a Christian on the chin, it tilts his face upward to look on the face of God.

2 Corinthians 4:1–18
v. 9

Jeremiah pronounced doom on the city of Babylon. The city, say the historians, was at this time one of the wonders of the ancient world. With its hanging gardens, its peacocks, its exquisite buildings and extravagant lifestyle, Babylon was the envy of the surrounding nations. Yet, when God decided to judge the city and bring about its destruction, there was nothing, or no one, that could save her.

Jeremiah 51:45–58

The Moffatt translation of verse 58 says that "pagans waste their pains". What an interesting phrase. The real thought here, of course, is that the pagans who built Babylon laboured in vain, because by their denial of God and His cause, they really got nowhere. The way Moffatt translates the verse suggests that the pagan men and women of Babylon failed to heed the warning signals of pain which God sent them, and thus, in the end, they were brought down.

Pain, as we know, is nature's warning bell which draws our attention to something wrong. If we see it as such we can profit from it, but if we ignore it, then we must accept the consequences. Ignoring pain is 'wasting' pain. I am speaking now not so much of physical pain as of the pain which unpleasant events and situations set up in the personality. How does a Christian deal with these pains? Instead of 'wasting' them, he uses them, sets them to music and makes them

sing. He is like the apple trees which, for some reason, when slashed produce finer and bigger apples. "For some reason," said a horticulturalist, "the trees bear better fruit when slashed and wounded in this way. So we slash them into added fruitfulness." So, my dear Christian friend, remember, the next time you are on the receiving end of an unpleasant situation or event, the 'slash' can become a reason for greater fruitfulness.

Are you, at this moment, a victim of someone's bitter and sarcastic tongue? It hurts, doesn't it? One can retaliate, of course, but recrimination is no way forward: it only increases the bitterness. Here's a better way – if you can do it: let the tongue-lashing slash you into fruitfulness. See the rebuff as an opportunity to smooth out the rough edges in your soul. The wound, strangely enough, brings healing.

Let no one think that what I am advocating is easy. No one likes to be treated with sarcasm and contempt. But the nearer we get to the spirit of Jesus Christ, and the more closely we inspect the principles of Scripture, the more we discover that there is a *better* way than retaliation – the way of making events make us. We may feel the pain, but instead of 'wasting' it, we accept it, and let it become a discipline for us – a discipline that makes us better in character and conduct. In other words, we take the pain and, with God's help, build a purpose into it. Pain that has no purpose in it is fruitless, it simply ends in suffering – and no more. But pain which has a purpose – or into which a purpose is built – contributes to the growth of the personality, and, in the end, greater spiritual fruitfulness.

Psalm 119:65–72
v. 71

A striking example of using situations to advance

God's purposes is seen when the Pharisees challenged Luke 6:1–11
Jesus about the Sabbath. Read Luke 6:1–11. The Living
Bible puts verse 11 like this: "At this, the enemies of v. 11
Jesus were wild with rage, and began to plot his
murder." How did Jesus react to that most difficult
situation? A few days later, we are told, He decided to
spend the whole night in prayer. What His thoughts
were during that night of prayer, we can only
conjecture, but I can't help feeling that, although He
knew that He was destined to die at Jerusalem, it must
have been borne home to Him that night in an even
more powerful way. He saw clearly that the opposition to
His ministry would eventually culminate in His death.
So before that happened, He decided that this would be
the moment at which He would choose the men who
would continue His ministry. When day broke, He
promptly proceeded to select the Twelve, the men who
would carry His message to the world when His own
mission had been fulfilled.

Here is a perfect example of what happens when God
works in someone whom He loves and who loves Him.
Such was Christ's love for His Father that He had
absolute trust in the Father's will. He knew that God
loved Him so much that He would allow nothing in His
life unless it furthered the purposes of their partnership.
And in the same way God wants to set up a similar
partnership in your life and mine. He pleads for our
absolute confidence and trust, so that whatever happens
we know that out of it will come a purpose that is wise
and good.

PRUNED ... BY LOSS

The last method of pruning we shall study together is the way God uses *circumstances of deprivation and loss* to further His purposes in our lives. We begin by focusing on the issue of *failure*. Some of our failures are due to the fact that we didn't try hard enough, didn't study hard enough, or didn't properly count the cost. Some failures, no doubt, are due to our physical condition – lack of energy, sickness, and so on. There are, indeed, many reasons for failure.

However, there are some failures which are deliberately engineered in heaven. They are brought about in the purposes of God for a very good reason. God often arranges for us to fail in a secondary thing that we might succeed in a primary thing. Many people are ruined by secondary successes. They become tangled up in them, and never get to the worthwhile things.

I am sure that God prevented me from achieving the success in engineering that I had set my eyes upon when I was a youth. I left college with good results, and was chosen from many applicants for an apprenticeship in a first-class engineering firm. But after a few years, the targets I had set for myself were not being achieved. I knew I could do it, but somehow things eluded me. One day I woke up and concluded that God wanted me to be an evangelist, not an engineer. My conclusion was right. I might have been crippled by a secondary success. At first I found it difficult to countenance the failure of my youthful ambitions, but now I am thankful for God's preventative grace.

Now we look at another condition of deprivation or loss – *cramped financial circumstances*. Are you in a

Philippians
1:12–26
v. 12

financial hole at the moment? It could be due, of course, to bad money management, inadequate budgeting, unemployment, sickness, or a dozen other things. But there are times when God takes a hand in our affairs, and gently squeezes us financially in order to get our attention more firmly fixed on Him.

Colossians 3:1–17
vv. 1–2

I once received a letter from a friend who said that he was going through a difficult time financially. He then said something which I asked his permission to share with you. He said: "Whenever I permit my spiritual affections to wander, God knows how to bring me to heel: He dries up the flow of my finances. Then it's not long before I am back at His feet, and pouring out my heart to Him in prayer."

I know many other Christians who have told me that one sure way for God to bring them into line is by bringing them into cramped financial circumstances. If you are having financial difficulties at this time (and keep in mind there could be other reasons than the one I have just mentioned), then reflect for a moment on your spiritual progress. Is God trying to get your attention in the only way He can – by drying up your finances? God doesn't delight in impoverishing us, but if we move toward being independent of Him, then low finances soon change our position.

Another circumstance of temporary deprivation and loss which God may bring about in the pruning process is *enforced inactivity*. I should point out, of course, that

Galatians
1:11–24

some inactivity is due to indisposition or other reasons, but what I am talking about here is the inactivity that comes because God has seemingly shut us up for a period of silence, where we appear to have no definite task to do for Him.   vv. 17–18

Sometimes our lives are so full of unprofitable activity that God has to put us on His 'unemployment list' so that we have time to listen to what He has to say to us. The temporary periods of being laid aside, of finding yourself without a task to do for Him, are sometimes part of His pruning purposes. If you are in such a condition at this moment, then it is important that you come before the Lord to find out the reasons for this enforced inactivity. If it is due to an obvious cause, such

as I have described earlier, then just rest in the fact that He is with you in the situation. But if it is due to some deficiency in you which God is trying, lovingly and gently, to prune from your life or character, then you need to ask Him to help you identify it.

Many of us become involved in endless activity in the Church, and take up every task given to us because it provides us with an escape route from our primary responsibilities. And what are they? Daily contact with God through prayer and the reading of His Word. If you don't have time for that, then you are far busier than God wants you to be. Sometimes we won't stop being active because we are afraid of what God might say to us when we come in silence before Him. I heard recently of a Christian woman, afflicted for many years with spinal trouble, who could not walk without crutches. One day as she was making her way downstairs, she slipped and fell to the bottom, her crutches remaining halfway up the stairs. She lay there for a long time, calling for help, but no one came. Eventually she said to herself, "This is ridiculous. I can't stay here all day." She pulled herself up and began to walk. And she has been walking ever since! The fall and the loss of those crutches was the best thing that could have happened to her.

There are many things in your life and mine, as we have been seeing, upon which we tend to lean heavily – success, money, friends, family, position. They may not be wrong, but they become crutches which weaken our moral fibre. We depend upon them too much. Then something happens, and they are taken away. At first we are stunned and crushed. Our crutches are gone – what's left? Why, our feet and our backbones, and the grace of God!

Hebrews 12:1–13

vv. 12–13